Bird Stencil Designs

Robert G. Bush

DOVER PUBLICATIONS, INC., *New York*

Published in Canada by General Publishing Company, Ltd., 30 Lesmill Road, Don Mills, Toronto, Ontario.
Published in the United Kingdom by Constable and Company, Ltd., 3 The Lanchesters, 162–164 Fulham Palace Road, London W6 9ER.

Bird Stencil Designs is a new work, first published by Dover Publications, Inc., in 1991.

DOVER *Pictorial Archive* SERIES

Manufactured in the United States of America
Dover Publications, Inc., 31 East 2nd Street, Mineola, N.Y. 11501

Library of Congress Cataloging-in-Publication Data

Bush, Robert G.
    Bird stencil designs / Robert G. Bush.
        p.   cm. — (Dover pictorial archive series)
        ISBN 0-486-26704-0 (pbk.)
        1. Stencil work—Themes, motives. 2. Birds in art. I. Title. II. Series.
    NK8655.B87   1991
    745.4—dc20   90-25814
                                                                            CIP

Publisher's Note

B IRD MOTIFS HAVE BEEN a perennial favorite among artists and decorators of all kinds. This striking assemblage of original stencil designs by noted California designer Robert G. Bush presents an extraordinary panorama of bird life, from seabirds like penguins and pelicans to exotic inhabitants of the tropics, such as birds of paradise, parrots and toucans. You will also find vigorous graphic interpretations of many other well-known types: ducks, cranes, flamingos, peacocks, pheasants and owls.

The designs are enhanced with stylized representations of branches and geometric figures, often recalling both Art Nouveau and Art Deco effects. Finally, many of the designs are repeated in varying sizes, multiple border and repeat patterns or "mirror-image" configurations—providing an even greater range of possible design applications.

3

4

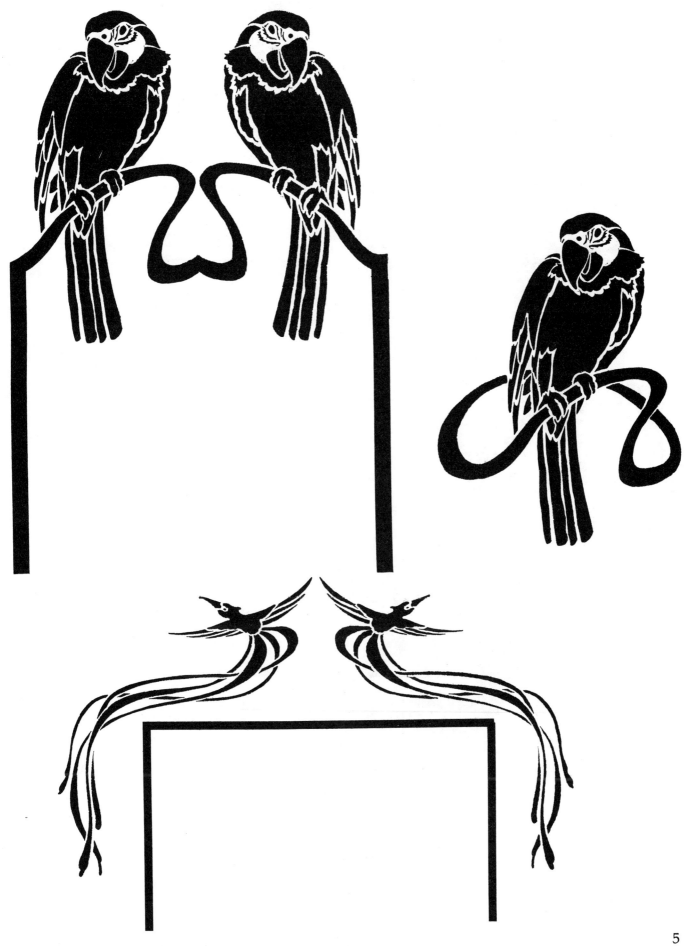

5

11

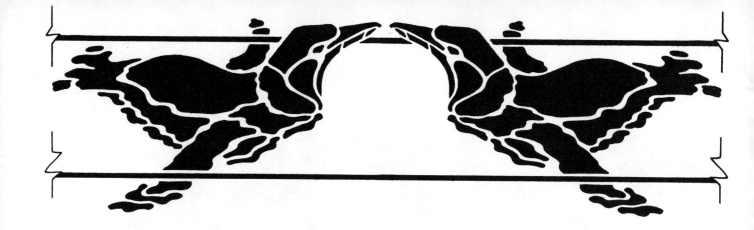

12

13

14

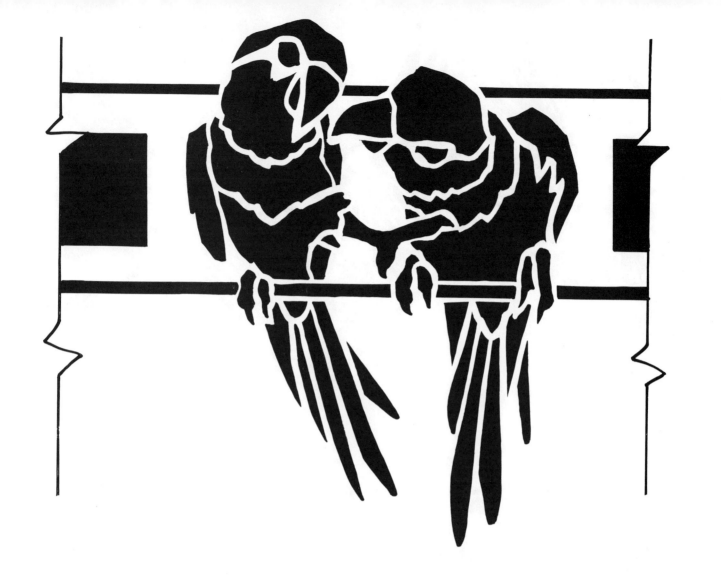

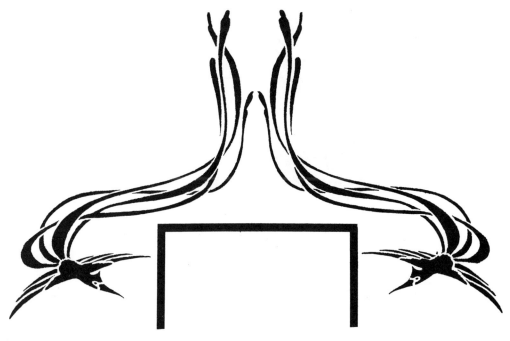

22

24

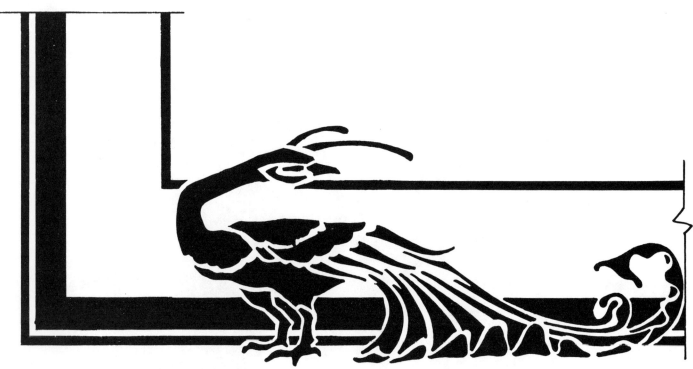

26

27

28

34

39

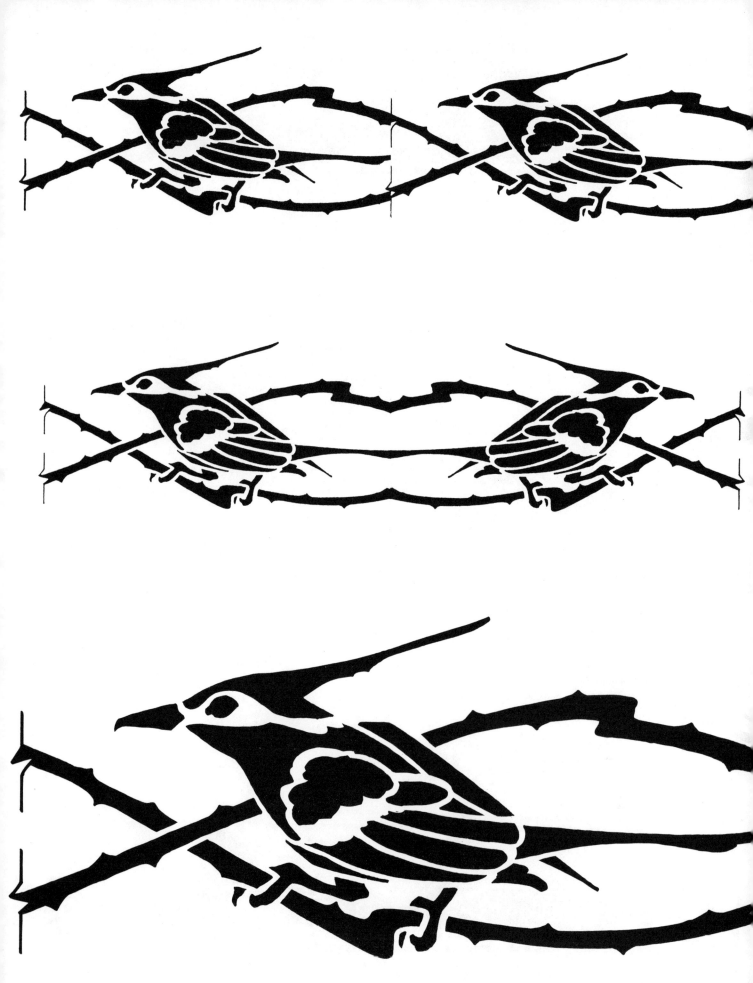

45

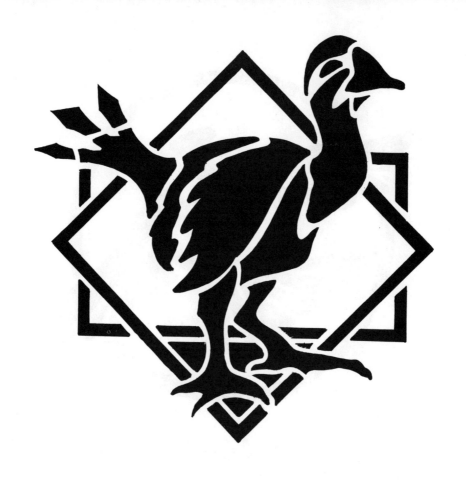

51

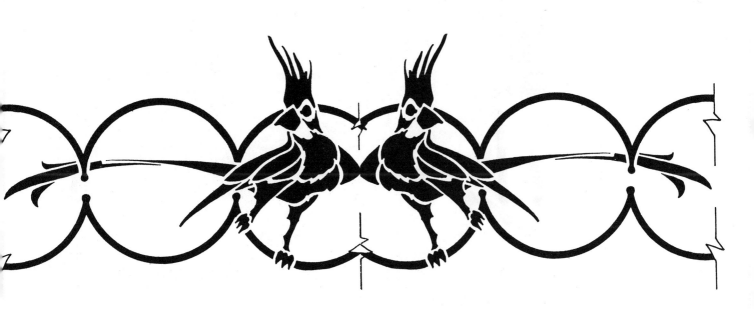

54

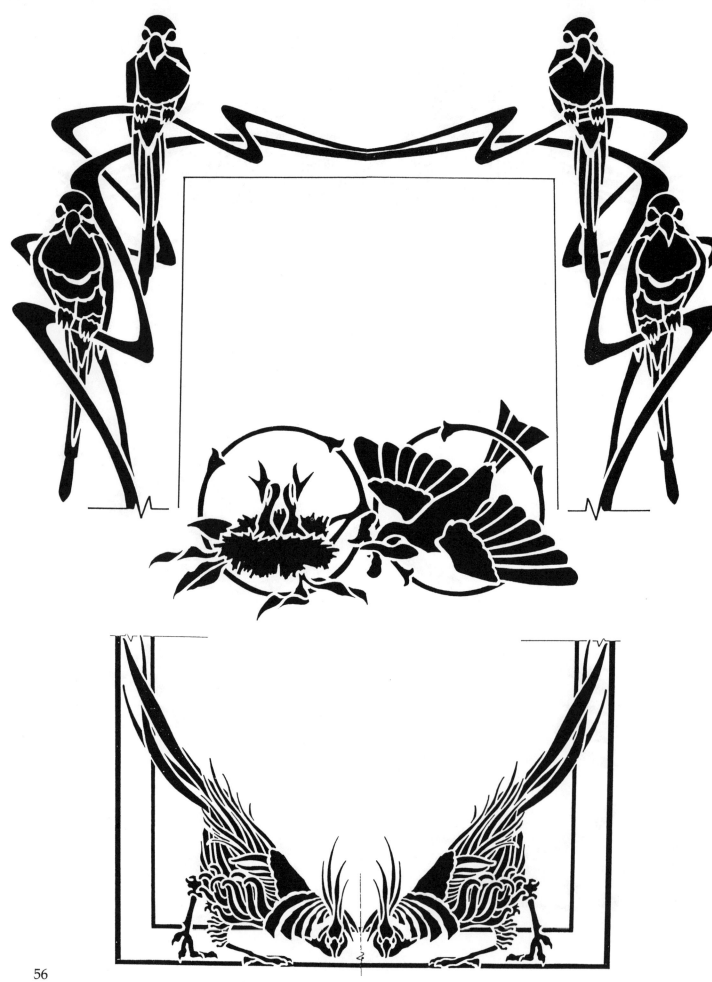

59